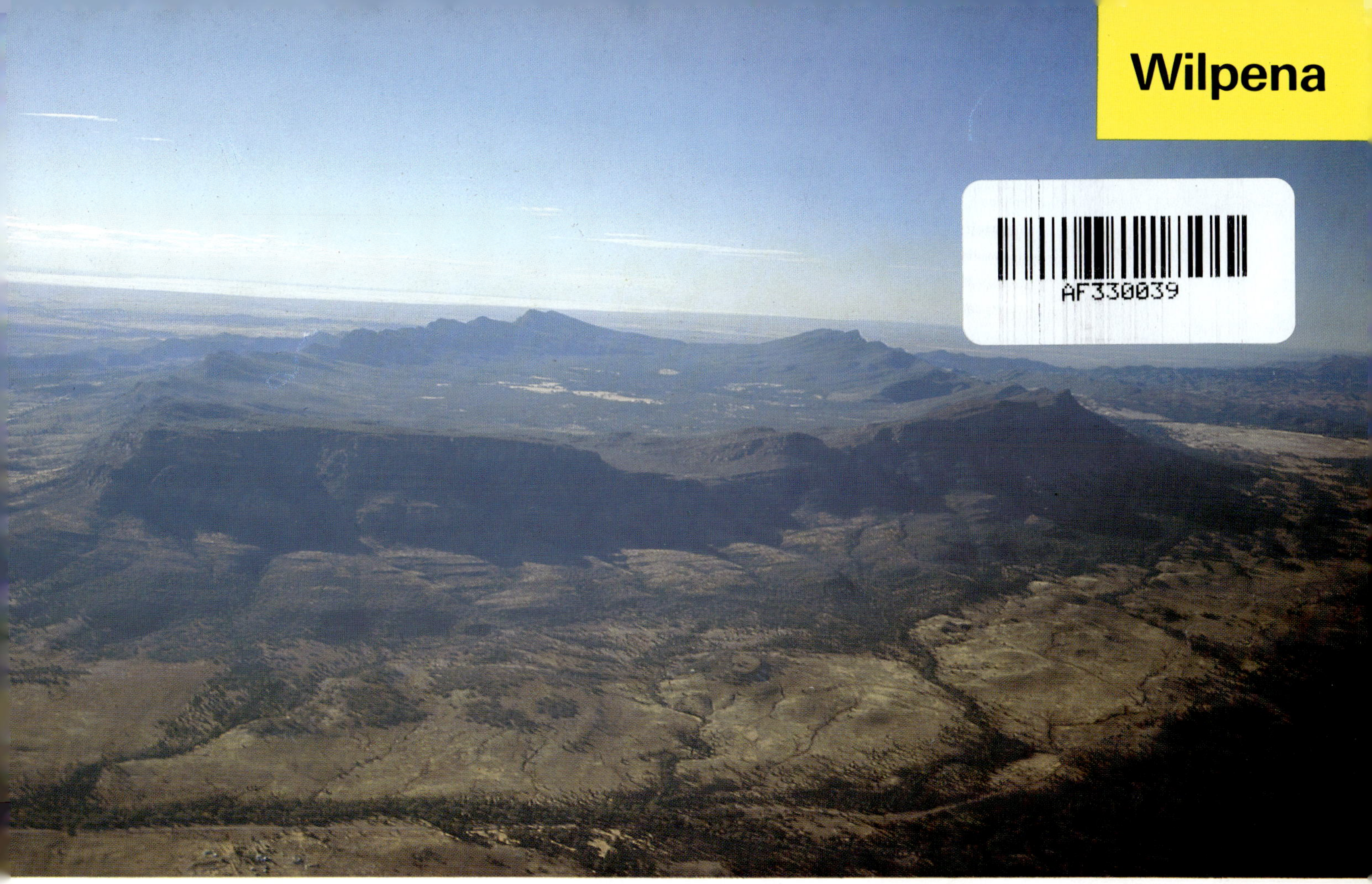

The best-known feature of the Flinders is Wilpena Pound (*above*), an immense elevated basin encircled by towering cliffs. The grandeur of this vast amphitheatre is best seen from the air. The sheer external cliffs rise to over 1000 metres (3300 feet), but inside they slope more gently to the floor of the plain. The changing colors of the Pound's walls and other spectacular rock formations in the Flinders have inspired many artists. The photograph (*right*) of the western facade of the Pound was taken at sunset when the walls glow with shades of pink, red and mauve.

Wilpena

Within the Pound are low rounded hills, folded ridges, grasslands and pine-clad slopes. The area abounds in bird-life. At the turn of the century, a farmer from Hawker, John Hill, grew wheat in the Pound and the remains of his stone homestead (*above left*) still stand. Hill constructed a road into the Pound which was destroyed by flood some years later. Today the only entrance to the Pound is through a narrow gorge and across Sliding Rock. Just outside the Pound is the small settlement of Wilpena. The resort (*above right*) caters for all levels of accommodation, from tents to a modern motel. A small airstrip (*left*) at Wilpena is used for scenic flights over the Pound and other local attractions.

From Wilpena, many tracks lead to a host of rugged gorges and beautiful valleys as well as to man-made attractions. At Rawnsley Park Station (*left*), south of Wilpena, demonstrations of sheep drafting and shearing are given at certain times of the year. Aboriginal paintings and carvings can be seen at Arkaroo Rock (*below right*) on the slopes of Rawnsleys Bluff, and at Sacred Canyon, just north of the entrance to Wilpena. The majestic St Mary's Peak (*below left*) is the highest part of the ramparts that surround the Pound. One of the many clearly marked walking tracks from Wilpena leads climbers to the summit of St Mary's Peak, from which a magnificent panorama of the Ranges can be seen.

Wilpena

The ruins of Appealinna homestead (*right*) are located north of Wilpena. The homestead was built in 1851 and sited on both sides of a tree-lined creek. All the buildings were constructed of flat rock, no mortar, taken from the creek bed. Other scenic attractions in the area include the Bunyeroo and Brachina Gorges. The Brachina Gorge (*below left*) slashes through the Heysen Range revealing richly colored rock faces. Delightful views of the Heysen Range can be seen along the Brachina-Bunyeroo road (*below right*).

Blinman (*above*) was a copper centre that boomed between 1860 and 1890. The population of Blinman during the prosperous 1870s was over 1000. Reminders of the boom days include the North Blinman Hotel built in 1865, which retains much of the atmosphere of the early outback, and an old miner's cottage (*right*) built in 1862. Today Blinman is a small town dependent on tourism for survival.

Blinman

The countryside around Blinman is magnificent particularly when the wild hops are in bloom. A scenic and interesting drive from Blinman is through the beautiful Aroona Valley (*above top*). The track meanders through the valley and leads to the ruin of the old Aroona Valley homestead. The road between Blinman and Oraparinna passes the Great Wall of China (*above left*) an impressive ironstone-capped ridge which runs parallel to the road for some distance at the top of a steep hill and bears a striking resemblance to the famous Chinese structure. Another delightful drive west of Blinman leads the visitor to the small town of Parachilna with its typical bush 'pub' (*above right*).

The road between Blinman and Parachilna winds through the superb Parachilna Gorge (*left*) and past many ideal spots for camping and picnicing. The beautiful Chambers Gorge (*below*) is located north-east of Blinman and is considered by many to be unequalled by anything else in the Flinders. Its charm lies in its isolation and its beauty. The area offers sparkling rock pools, Aboriginal carvings and prolific bird-life. Just north of Chambers Gorge is the spectacular Big Moro Gorge with its rugged cliffs and numerous rock pools.

Hawker

Hawker, established in 1880, was once an important town due to the north-south railway which passed through the settlement. The old station yards (*left*) are well worth looking over. The railway line now bypasses the town, but Hawker has remained a major centre for the Flinders because of its position at the junction for all roads leading north. Hawker today offers the traveller modern motels, a caravan park, a wide range of shopping facilities and a museum. For the sporting enthusiast Hawker has a golf course (*below*), swimming pool, bowling green and tennis courts.

opposite: The Moralana Scenic Drive, considered to be one of the highlights of the Flinders, links the main Parachilna and Blinman Roads north of Hawker. The road winds through part of the Elder Range, also known as the Hills of Arkaba, a name made famous by the paintings of Sir Hans Heysen. At one stage the road climbs a ridge offering magnificent views of the Elder Range and Wilpena Pound.

Hawker

Aboriginal Art

There were several Aboriginal tribes in the Flinders Ranges when the first settlers arrived. Their past presence is evidenced today by the remains of Aboriginal art painted or carved centuries ago throughout the Ranges. Rock carvings can be seen at Chambers Gorge (*right above*) north-east of Blinman and also at Sacred Canyon (*right below*) near Wilpena. Aboriginal drawings and paintings can be viewed at Yourambulla Cave, south of Hawker, and at Arkaroo Rock on the eastern slope of Wilpena Range.

South of Hawker is the Kanyaka Death Rock (*left above*) which overlooks a permanent waterhole. This area was once an Aboriginal ceremonial ground. Nearby are the ruins of Kanyaka (*left below*), once a thriving, industrious community supporting over seventy men and their families from the 1850s to the 1870s. A roadside inn was built near the homestead and around this a town was surveyed in 1863. Later the Great Northern, a two-storied, twenty-roomed hotel was built and traded till 1881. The railway, built in 1880, bypassed the town and the loss of through traffic and adverse seasons caused the settlement to die. The ruins of the homestead and the graveyard are all that remain today.

The Flinders are at their best in Spring especially after good rains when the display of wildflowers is breathtaking. The whole region is carpeted with every imaginable color including the brilliant red of wildhops (*above*) and the purple of Salvation Jane (*left*). The vivid colors of the wildflowers are complemented by the grey-green of the river red gums (*opposite*), which follow the courses of the generally dry creeks, and the steel-blue foliage of the native pines, which often occur in extensive picturesque stands.

Flora

Quorn

The township of Quorn nestles in a valley in the southern Flinders. It serves as a shopping centre for local pastoralists and its 'old pioneer' atmosphere is popular with tourists. The town offers excellent accommodation, a bowling green, tennis courts and a swimming pool. Quorn has many old buildings including the public school and railway station, both built in 1880. The Quorn Mill (*right above*) was built in 1878 to grind the wheat yield but unreliable rainfall forced this industry to be abandoned and the mill became redundant. The building is now a motel, restaurant, art gallery and museum. Just south of Quorn the road leads to colorful Devil's Peak (*right below*), a forbidding feature that overlooks Quorn and which offers enjoyable bushwalking and excellent panoramic views.

Visitors to Quorn during holiday periods can take a ride on the Pichi Richi train (*left above*) through the Pichi Richi Pass (*left below*). Quorn was established as a railway town in 1878 and developed into an important railway junction. However a broad gauge railway line was built on the western plains and the Pichi Richi line closed in 1957. A preservation society was formed and it restored the old line, obtained steam engines and rolling stock and re-opened the line in 1974. There is also a road that runs through the Pichi Richi Pass offering travellers many delightful picnic spots and magnificent views.

North of Quorn are the picturesque Warren Gorge (*above*), popular with climbing enthusiasts, and the Buckaringa Gorge (*right*) with its scenic picnic areas. Near the turn-off to Buckaringa Gorge a road leads to the grave of Hugh Proby, founder of Kanyaka station, who was drowned at the age of twenty-four while crossing the flooded Willochra Creek on horseback in 1852.

Wilmington is a tiny settlement south of Quorn whose main attraction is the Mount Remarkable National Park nearby. The Park is famous for its crystal pools, dense vegetation and abundant wildlife. Located in the Park is the majestic Alligator Gorge (*above left*) with its impressive rock formations, sparkling mountain pools and prolific ferns. Horrocks Pass (*above right*) is one of the few passes through the southern Flinders and is on the road between Wilmington and Port Augusta. Nearby is Hancocks Lookout (*left*) which offers excellent views over the surrounding country to Spencer Gulf.

Melrose

Melrose (*above*), the oldest town in the Flinders Ranges, is a quiet, attractive town that lies at the foot of Mount Remarkable. The more energetic who climb the mount are rewarded with stunning views of the surrounding area. Melrose boasts some lovely old buildings, including the old Police Station and Courthouse (*right*), built in 1862 and now a National Trust Museum. The display includes many historical exhibits of early settlement.

Wildlife throughout the Flinders is abundant. Small parties of red kangaroos can be seen feeding or bounding across the plains or the grasslands of the valleys. In the more elevated areas, euros or hill kangaroos can be found, while in the more remote rocky gullies the rare and beautiful yellow-footed rock wallaby (*above left*) can be seen. On the plains, particularly when the grass is seeding, large flocks of galahs (*above right*), corellas and finches abound. Also seen frequently on the plains and in the more open country are emus (*left*). Cormorants, swans, ducks, herons and other water-birds congregate around the permanent water-holes.

Leigh Creek

Leigh Creek is the largest town between Port Augusta and Alice Springs. Its economy is based on the large open-cut coalfields (*right above*) which supply coal for the power station at Port Augusta. The residents of Leigh Creek were moved in 1982 to a new town, as the site of the original township was needed for further mining operations. The town of Copley (*right below*), south of Leigh Creek, marks the turn-off to Arkaroola which lies to the east.

South of Leigh Creek is the Aroona Dam (*left above*) located in a steep-sided valley with richly colored walls. The dam was built to supply water to the town and the coalfields. Still further south lies the old railway township of Beltana (*left below*). Here many of the old buildings have been restored including the railway station, pictured, which now houses a museum and general store. East of Beltana, the remains of the Sliding Rock mining community can be seen.

Arkaroola

The remote village settlement of Arkaroola (*right above*) was founded in 1968 and offers motel accommodation, and a caravan and camping area. It is part of a flora and fauna sanctuary known as the Arkaroola-Mount Painter Sanctuary which covers an extremely rugged and beautiful area of the northern Flinders. The region is a museum of natural history containing some of the oldest rocks in the Flinders, a range of minerals not found elsewhere and a wealth of scenery and wildlife. Near Arkaroola are the remains of the Bolla Bollana copper mines (*right below*). The smelter round-house still stands but the main smelter and chimney, pictured, now lie in ruins. Most of the history of the area is bound up in mining, mainly copper, which began in the 1860s and had ceased by the turn of the century.

Arkaroola

The rugged, arid mountains found in the Arkaroola-Mount Painter region are geologically of great antiquity. The oldest rocks in the Ranges occur in the Arkaroola-Mount Painter region known as the Freeling Heights (*left*) and date back some 1600 million years. The Paralana Hot Springs (*below*), just north of Arkaroola, are unique as they are believed to be the last vestige of volcanic activity in Australia. The area is an ancient Aboriginal ceremonial site and has been proclaimed an historic reserve.

Arkaroola

Guided tours of the rugged heartland are available from Arkaroola and one of the most popular is the famous ridgetop tour. A convoy of four-wheel drive vehicles takes visitors along narrow trails that scramble over mountains, along razor-back ridges and plummet periodically to cool valleys and gorges. Highlights of this tour include startling rock formations like Split Rock (*above left*), Mount Painter (*right*), the site of Australia's first uranium mine, Mount Gee (an amazing mountain of quartz crystals) and the unforgettable view across mountain tops to Lake Frome and beyond from Sillers Lookout (*above right*).